Designed for Plunder

How the Federal Reserve Took Your House, Job, and Savings

Richard Walbaum

ISBN-10: 1475241798
ISBN-13: 978-1475241792

Rev. 050212

www.NaturalLawRemedy.com

Also by Richard Walbaum: *The LAWFUL Remedy to Tyranny*

Table of Contents

Introduction

Everything in Creation occurs in great abundance. Innumerable galaxies and stars, six billion people (too many to count), there is no shortage of anything. The Nature of life itself seems to be abundance.

If abundance is natural, why do many people experience poverty, and struggle to make ends meet? Why was one breadwinner enough in the 1950s, two required in the 80's, and two not enough in the 90s?

For eight years I studied the cause of poverty. I read the success books, the "You can do it!" types of books, I also studied economics, learned how money was created and placed into circulation, and I studied law. Then one day the pieces of my eight year quest came together to unfold the secret of the universe:

The reason there is lack of money when the nature of life is abundance, is because nature is abundant, but money isn't!

Money is not abundant because it is created by a system whose main *virtue* is it creates universal poverty. Then there are its vices which soon you will discover.

This is not a success book. The problem is not where you think it is, the solution is not what you think it might be, and I am going to give you answers to questions that you probably never asked.

This book will show you why the design of our monetary system is responsible for appropriating the wealth away from the American people. The entire field of economics is so muddled you can get a PhD and still not know what you are talking about. I asked an economics professor from a local university to read the first three chapters of this book which explain the problem of our monetary system. He literally said "I agree with what you have written, but where is the problem?" Such an answer remains one of life's mysteries to me that minds can work so differently, for the problem is clearly explained. Other economists give similar unsatisfying answers. Perhaps economists minds are scrambled.

I am an electronics engineer by profession. Automatic control systems are necessary to land unmanned craft on Mars, or maintain constant price levels. To engineers, control system theory[1] is very mature and well understood, but judging by the results, economists do not use or understand it. When I see a system with a rising exponential (a mathematical property) in it, I call the system "unstable; going to crash"; economists call it "compound interest." A system that oscillates is unstable; economists call this a "business cycle." I can see why economics is often called the "dismal" science.

Usury (generally the loaning of money at interest) creates many problems, and for that reason was forbidden in the past.[2] I believe that any society that practices usury will be destroyed by it. Historians theorize the fall of empires due to various reasons; usury should be the first cause to look for.

If you have taken economics from the government schools, you will probably see usury to be benevolent. They will explain the time value of money, and how people should be paid for the loss of the use of money that is loaned.[3] Most of the world's monetary systems are based on usury which doesn't make it right, but only makes the problems more widespread and severe. When you are done reading you will gain a perspective that you were not taught in school that will explain why the world has so many problems and countries are on the verge of bankruptcy. There are practical alternatives to usury described in this book.

This book was originally published in 1994; the principles are the same, though the numbers may be different. Whenever [brackets] appear, they are my words, not those of the quotation.

---

1   See http://en.wikipedia.org/wiki/Control_system and http://en.wikipedia.org/wiki/Control_theory.
2   See these Biblical anti-usury Statutes: Exodus 22:25; Leviticus 25:13-16, 25:23, 25:29-31, and 25:36-37; Deuteronomy 23:19-20; Proverbs 28:8. The Bible is not a book of economics and doesn't explain why usury is evil and why it is forbidden, nor would the common people of the times necessarily understand an explanation.
3   See http://en.wikipedia.org/wiki/Opportunity_cost.

Chapter 1

How Money Is Created In the United States

How would you like a monetary system that seems like a fairy tale where money almost grows on trees, the Government never has to borrow, prices are stable, and it all is based on sound mathematical principles? I want you to know that a sound monetary system is possible and there are solutions to our economic problems.

This chapter will describe where our money comes from. You will learn how the Federal Reserve creates money, and how the commercial banks create even more money using "fractional reserve debt expansion." The next chapter will elaborate why most of our problems (including rising prices) are caused by a system design error.[4] The third chapter will look at one possible monetary system that will support unbridled prosperity and heaven on earth. The fourth chapter will take a step back to define money and its various embodiments, along with their benefits and problems. There can be no doubt that nature is abundant in every area; money can be abundant as well if we choose it.

---

4   The word "error" implies a mistake. Historically, it was done intentionally, with malice aforethought. For a history of the Federal Reserve, see *The Secrets of the Federal Reserve*, Eustace Mullins, Bankers Research Institute, P.O. Box 1105, Staunton, VA 24401, 1985. The inside story of who runs and owns the Federal Reserve. As told in the forward to the book, after researching and writing up his work on the Federal Reserve, Mr. Mullins:

"... began efforts to market this manuscript in New York. Eighteen publishers turned it down, but the nineteenth ... gave me some friendly advice in his office. 'I like your book, but we can't print it. Neither can anybody else in New York. ... You may as well forget about getting the Federal Reserve book published. I doubt if it could ever be printed.'"

This book is available free online at www.apfn.org/apfn/reserve.htm. This book I could not read in one sitting; it was so depressing I had to put it down from time to time.

Death, Taxes, and Other Myths

There are two constants in life: Death and taxes. Right? Some of us believe that death can be beat; but taxes? How could a government run without income taxes? Did you know that we did fine without personal income taxes until the early part of the 1900s, and that government funding was via duties and excises?[5]

How about banks? Banks take the money you deposit and loan it to others, right? Wrong. The fact is, the money loaned to others is created by the banks and did not exist before the loan was made. People generally believe that the purpose of a bank is a convenient place to store your money. In fact, this is a secondary function. The primary function of a bank is to create money.

Finally, price inflation is caused by the government printing the money to pay its bills, right? Wrong. The last time the government paid its bills by printing money was in 1862 when Lincoln issued Greenbacks to pay for the Civil War.[6]

The Federal Reserve: The Fourth Branch of Government

There are three branches of government: Executive, Legislative, and Judicial, right? As a practical matter, I suggest that there is a hidden fourth branch called the Federal Reserve.[7]

The Federal Reserve (Fed) is an agency created by Congress by the Federal Reserve Act of 1913. Its purpose is to control the quantity, cost, and availability of money. It is the sovereign prime money-creating authority, and is solely responsible for increasing or decreasing its supply.

---

5   "[The] original expectation was that the power of direct taxation would be exercised only in extraordinary exigencies, and down to August 15, 1894, this expectation has been realized." *Pollock v. Farmers' Loan & Trust*, 157 U.S. 429, 574 (1895). Whether or not today's income tax is direct or indirect (the definition is cloudy), it has the bite of a direct tax, and this type of tax has been avoided until the early 1900s:
"[U]ntil the past few years, the United States has generally been able to obtain all needful revenue from the single source of duties upon imports." [*Pollock*, supra, 623; quoting Pomeroy's Constitutional Law (Sec 281); no date].

6   The Act of February 25, 1862 authorized the issue of $150,000,000 in Legal Tender United States Notes. [*The Story of Our Money*, Olive Cushing Dwinell, Boston: Forum Publishing Co., 1946, p. 112]. The total issue was $449,338,902 which was spent into circulation directly by the U.S. Government, and not subject to either interest or debt. [*The Truth In Money Book*, Thoren and Warner, Truth in Money, Inc., 1985, (P.O. Box 30, Chagrin Falls, Ohio 44022) p.135]

7   For more information and citations, see http://www.wanttoknow.info/financialbankingcoverup.

The Fed is made up of three parts. The first part is the Board of Governors, a quasi-government agency that sets economic policy independently of the President, Congress, and the Supreme Court; they counsel or make suggestions, but they do not control. It was intentionally set up this way to remove economic policy from the tides of political change, but it also removed it from representative government. The Fed, though independent of government control, has the power of a separate major branch of government.

The board consists of seven persons, appointed by the President of the United States and confirmed by the Senate, for fourteen year terms. The terms are staggered, so that one term expires every two years. The long terms and staggered appointments are designed to produce a Federal Reserve System independent of other branches and agencies of the government.[8]

Just as the Congress represents the will of the people, the Fed represents the will of Congress. If Congress doesn't like monetary policy, they can pass legislation, or convince the president to appoint new governors to represent them, but only one new governor every two years.

The second part is composed of 12 regional Federal Reserve banks:

The 12 Regional Reserve Banks aren't government institutions but corporations nominally "owned" by member commercial banks, who must buy special, non-marketable stock in their district Federal Reserve Bank.[9]

To demonstrate that regional Reserve banks are privately owned (don't let "Federal" fool you), the 12 regional Federal Reserve Banks pay real estate tax, their employees are not in Civil Service, and they are not listed under "U.S. Government" in the phone books (unlike government agencies).[10] But, the Reserve Banks do perform important governmental functions which make them federal instrumentalities.[11]

---

8   *Putting it simply ... The Federal Reserve*, Federal Reserve Bank of Boston, 1984, p.5.
9   *I bet you thought...*, David H. Friedman, Federal Reserve Bank of New York (1984) p. 21.
     The Federal Reserve is owned by The Rothschild Bank of London and Berlin; Kuhn, Loeb Co.;
     Lazard Freres of Paris (a Rothschild spinoff); Warburg Bank of Hamburg, Germany, and Amsterdam,
     The Netherlands; Lehman Brothers Bank of New York; Israel Moses Seif Banks of Italy; Goldman,
     Sachs Bank of New York; and Chase Manhattan Bank of New York (a Rockefeller bank).
     They own special stock that pays a 6% dividend. This stock is unlike ordinary stock; it is not a
     claim of ownership, it cannot be sold or pledged for loans, and it carries no voting rights. [*The Federal
     Reserve Scandal!*, Hargis and Sampson, New Leaf Press, Inc., Green Forest, AR 72638, 1984, p. 37-38]
10   *Figuring out the Fed*, Margaret Thoren, Truth in Money, Inc., 1985, (P.O. Box 30, Chagrin falls,
     Ohio, 44022), p. 4-5.
11   "The test for determining whether an entity is a federal instrumentality for purposes of protection
     from state and local action or taxation, however is very broad: whether the entity performs an
     important governmental function." [*Lewis v. United States*, 680 F. 2d 1239, 1242 (1982)]

These 12 Reserve Banks act collectively like a central bank which holds the accounts of all the commercial banks; this allows transactions between commercial member banks to be easily accomplished. They also perform as a check clearing house. A check deposited in one bank usually goes through one or more Fed banks on its way back to the bank it was written on.

The third part is the 5,425 Federal Reserve System member banks, out of the 15,171 commercial banks (as of 1979).

The Open Market Committee is sometimes considered a fourth part of the system.

How the Fed Controls the Money Supply

The Fed has three tools with which to control the money supply. First, the Fed can adjust the discount rate which is the interest rate at which member banks can borrow funds from the Fed. It is called a "discount" because the interest is paid (discounted) at the time the loan is made.

Second, the Fed can adjust the reserve requirement which determines the amount of money a commercial bank can create. The general public thinks of the "reserves" as a store of funds to be used in case of shortage or emergency. For banks, "reserves" are not a reserve or storage; reserves are the base upon which new money is created.

Third, the Fed can buy or sell Treasury bonds (government debt) thereby increasing or decreasing the money supply directly; this is called "Open Market Operations."

Changes in the reserve requirement or discount rate are long term controls. These play a secondary role to Open Market Operations which we will now concern ourselves with.

Congress chose to execute its power of Article 1 Section 8 Clause 5 (To coin money, [and] regulate the value thereof...), by using corporations:

That wherever a legislature has the right to accomplish a certain result, and that result is best attained by means of a corporation, it has the right to create such a corporation, and to endow it with the powers necessary to effect the desired and lawful purpose, seems hardly to admit of debate. [*Slaughter House Cases*, 16 Wall 36, 64 (1872)]

The Fed Creates Money Whenever It Buys

The Fed creates money whenever it buys anything. Being the sovereign money creating authority, it never has to borrow. Suppose the Fed buys $1 million of Treasury bonds by writing a check to a dealer (see Figure 1.1).

Figure 1.1: Tracing the Flow of Money Created by the Federal Reserve

Follow the circled steps in the diagram.

Step 1: The Fed writes a check of $1 million out of thin air. This creates money because, unlike personal checks, there is no money on deposit to cover the check.

Step 2: The Fed gives the Securities Dealer the check, and the Dealer gives the Fed a security.

Step 3: The Dealer deposits the check in his bank, and the bank credits his account by $1 million.

Step 4: The bank sends the check to the Fed for payment, who credits the bank's account by $1 million.

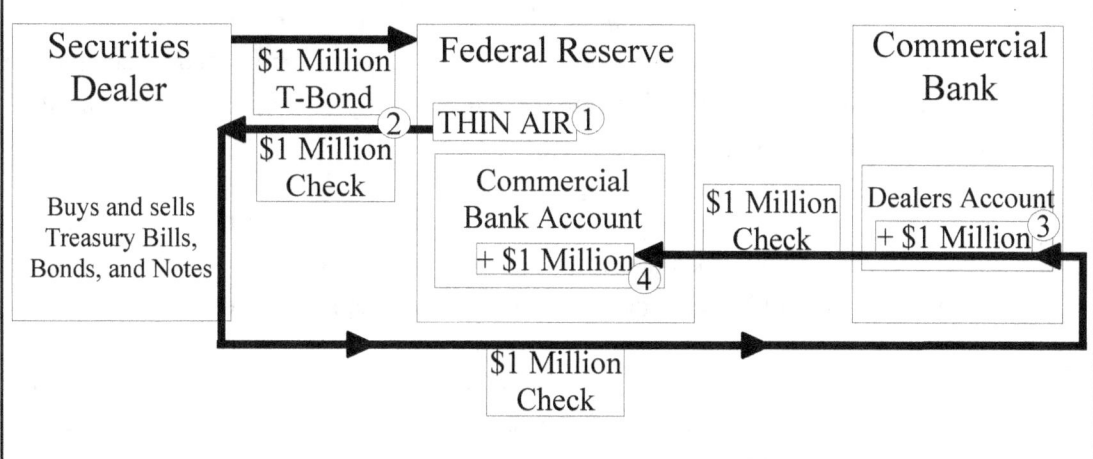

The dealer deposits the check in a local bank, and the bank returns it to the Fed for payment. The Fed "pays" the check by crediting the bank's reserve account by simple bookkeeping entries. These reserves are as good as cash to the bank. This cost the Fed nothing since no account is debited, but $1 million of new money is put into circulation (the dealer has it on deposit at the bank).

The Fed destroys money whenever it sells anything. By selling bonds, the reverse process takes place, and the money supply is decreased. As of 1984, the Fed held about $160 billion of government securities that it could sell.[12]

The Banks Create Money by Making Loans

Modern banking developed from the goldsmiths. To protect their gold from theft, people would deposit their gold with the goldsmiths for safekeeping. The goldsmith would issue them receipts. People would use these receipts for money because they were confident that the receipts could be redeemed for gold at any time.[13]

The goldsmiths discovered that only a small portion of their gold was ever demanded, and they started issuing more receipts than they had gold. The goldsmiths could issue receipts valued at about ten times the gold they had on hand, and thereby make ten times more interest on the money created. Thus was born "fractional reserve banking." The banker today creates money just like the goldsmith did, but the details are different.

Currency is the modern day equivalent of gold; when the banker creates money he must be able to pay currency on demand. Thus, it is the currency on hand that limits how much money today's banker can create, just as gold limited how many receipts the goldsmith could issue. Instead of circulating warehouse receipts, banks circulate checkbook money (bank bookkeeping entries).

A bank creates money whenever it makes a loan. When you borrow money from a bank, the money you borrow does not exist prior to your borrowing it; the bank creates the money by simply crediting your account, using bookkeeping entries.

The bank must be careful when it creates bookkeeping entries so that it will have sufficient cash in reserve to cash checks. For every $100 the bank creates by crediting your account with bookkeeping entries, it must have an average of $10 on hand to cash checks on demand. Thus, it is the cash on hand (and on deposit at the Fed) that limits the amount of money a bank can create.

---

12 *I bet you thought...*, Federal Reserve Bank of New York, 1984, p. 23.
13 *Modern Money Mechanics*, Federal Reserve Bank of Chicago, 1982, p. 3-4

The whole system is based on the fact that, on the average, people will keep most of their money in the form of checking accounts (bookkeeping entries), and only a small portion in cash.

Suppose the Fed creates money by buying securities, and $2 million of this finds its way into a bank. See Figure 1.2. The bank does *not* loan this money out; it is placed in the vault, or deposited with the regional Federal Reserve bank. It is kept as "reserves," on the basis of which the bank will create more money (by simply using a sharp pencil to credit the customers accounts).

The bank wants to create money because the bank makes 10 times more interest on $20 million of loans then it does on $2 million. However, it cannot make a single loan of $20 million to a single customer because if the customer tries to cash the check, the bank will only be able to pay $2 million of it.

On the other hand, the bank can make 2,000 loans of $10,000 each (a total of $20 million in loans) with only a $2 million reserve. This is because, on the average, the customers will cash less than 10% of the $20 million. In this way the $2 million of cash in the bank will be sufficient reserves for the $20 million the bank loans out.

Figure 1.2: Example of How the Banks Create Money

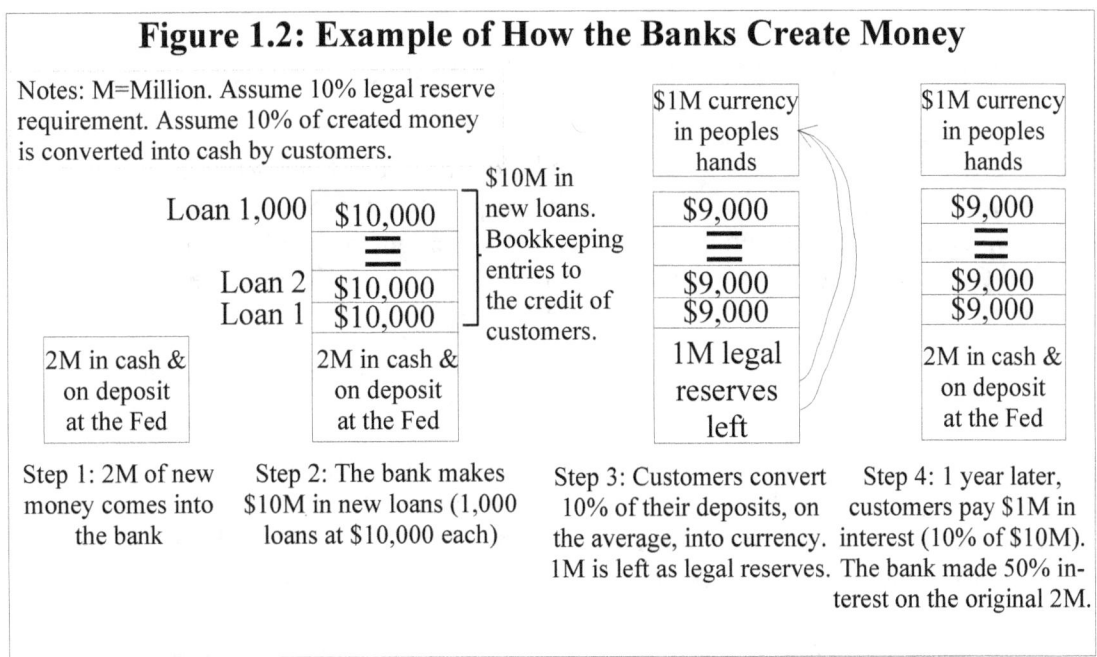

Notes: M=Million. Assume 10% legal reserve requirement. Assume 10% of created money is converted into cash by customers.

Step 1: 2M of new money comes into the bank

Step 2: The bank makes $10M in new loans (1,000 loans at $10,000 each)

Step 3: Customers convert 10% of their deposits, on the average, into currency. 1M is left as legal reserves.

Step 4: 1 year later, customers pay $1M in interest (10% of $10M). The bank made 50% interest on the original 2M.

But the bank is not allowed to use the entire $2 million to create $20 million. With a 10% "reserve requirement" set by the Fed, the bank is required to keep $10 in cash reserve for every $100 it creates. The best this bank can do is keep $1 million as reserves to create $10 million (since the other $1 million is "cashed" by the customers).[14] This process of creating a multiple of deposited money is called "fractional reserve debt expansion."[15] The created money is also called a "deposit" because it is deposited in customers accounts.

Whatever amount of money is placed into circulation by the Fed will eventually be expanded by the banking system. Conversely, whatever money is removed from circulation by the Fed will eventually be contracted by the banking system.

Mathematically, the money supply can expand or contract by 100 divided by the reserve requirement: 100 / 10% = 10 times. A 15% reserve requirement would allow the money supply to be multiplied by 100 / 15% = 6.67 times.

The reserve requirement varies depending on the type of deposit and the size of bank. Time deposits may be as low as 3%; checking deposits may be around 15%.

Robert Owen, former Chairman, Committee on Banking and Currency, United States Senate, gave an example of how banks create money:

> [T]he prime object of the banker was to make a loan that was safe, that would pay him the legal rate of interest, and that would be paid at a fixed period of time.

> Mr. John Smith wanted a thousand dollars against security. Mr. Smith would give his note for 90 days, bearing 6-percent interest, with the security attached. And the banker would thereupon enter on the books of the bank a credit to John Smith, precisely as if John Smith had paid into the bank that amount in gold dollars, or in legal-tender notes.

> The banker and John Smith combined in this way to create a demand bank deposit subject to check.

> When John Smith made this contract with the bank, the bank agreed to pay his checks on demand in legal tender to the extent of the loan. Here was the manufacture of money in the form of a demand bank deposit by John Smith and the bank. Thus public and private assets were monetized by the bank.

---

14 Traditional charts show how the banking system as a whole, multiplies the money based on reserves; I show the esoteric method in which one bank can multiply the money, just like the goldsmiths. See *Modern Money Mechanics*.

15 Explained in the booklet *Modern Money Mechanics*, Federal Reserve Bank of Chicago, 1982 (P.O. Box 834, Chicago Illinois 60690). Also available everywhere on the internet.

Not only was money thus created by the bank and its depositors, but the money supply of the country was contracted when the loan was paid off.[16]

Money is not Created by Printing It

Money comes in two forms: Currency (including coins), and bank deposits (bookkeeping entries). About 70% of our money is held as bank deposits; 27% is paper currency, and 3% is coin.[17]

Whether money is held as bank deposits or currency is entirely up to consumer choice or demand. If currency is demanded, the Fed buys the currency from the Treasury for the price of paper, ink, and printing, and sells it to the commercial banks. A bill of any denomination costs about 2 cents.

True money creation is done by bookkeeping entries by the Fed and the commercial banks. It is converted into currency only as a convenience to customers. Customers buy currency from the bank in exchange for bookkeeping entries.

Checks Function as Money

Robert Owen explained:

Checks function as money. They represent money. They are safeguarded against counterfeiting by law. They are safeguarded against fraud. They comprise the greatest medium of exchange and measure of value in the United States, their volume reaching the colossal figure in 1929 of $1,230,000,000,000. They transact over 95 percent of the monetary business of the United States; and even the currency which is employed by the people is usually obtained by cashing a check in the bank and converting the check into legal tender money.[18]

In the next chapter you will discover how one design flaw is the cause of virtually all of our problems. Handle this one problem and all the rest disappear, like magic!

---

16   Robert Owen, *National Economy and the Banking System*, Senate Document #23, 1939, p.15.
17   *I bet you thought...*, Federal Reserve Bank of New York, 1984, p. 5.
18   Robert Owen, *National Economy and the Banking System*, Senate Document #23, 1939, p. 8.

Chapter 2

Our Monetary System Has a Design Error

In the first chapter we learned the surprising facts about how money was created by the Federal Reserve (Fed) and the commercial banks. Its purpose was to prepare you for this chapter which shows that our entire money supply is *loaned* into circulation, and unpayable interest on the money supply gives rise to most of the problems we are experiencing.

Why a Balanced Budget Will Not Prevent Increasing Debt

The reason we have a $3 trillion national debt and $8 trillion private debt is because people, government, and business have spent beyond their means, right? Wrong. The fact is, our monetary system guarantees that debt must increase regardless of what people, business or government do or do not do, whether or not they balance their budgets.

Suppose I loan you 10 Picassos (rare paintings), the very last 10 in existence, with the condition that you return 10 to me plus one more Picasso as interest. If you knew there were only 10 in existence, you would not accept this offer, but suppose you are naive about the creation and circulation of Picassos and you accept the terms; when repayment time comes, you only possess 10, having been unable to get the non-existent 11th Picasso. You lose your house which was pledged as collateral. A silly story you say, no one would do that. Don't be so sure; our monetary system works the same way!

Another example: Suppose you deposit $1,000 into a bank at 10% compound annual interest, which means that each year you will make interest on the interest. In 145 years you will have over $1 billion, an exponential growth of 1,000,000 times.[19] The moral: A small amount, held as a perpetual debt, quickly compounds to astronomical amounts.

Our money supply was loaned into existence, and you don't pay back a money supply. Compound interest payments will cause this debt to rise to astronomical amounts (it already has). Furthermore, just like my Picassos example, there is always more debt than there is money to pay it back, so it can never be paid back (the best we can do is refinance it). This is why I said that balancing the Federal budget is irrelevant.

Our Money Supply is One Big Debt

In Chapter 1 we learned that the Fed creates money by writing checks (against no funds) to buy Treasury bills from securities dealers, and this money makes its way into the commercial banks who multiply this money – create new money by making loans to customers using bookkeeping entries. Now lets see how the money supply is created by the banks:

> Deposit creation [bookkeeping money created by the banks], rather than currency deposits, accounts for most of the $375 billion of checkbook money. Banks hold only about $40 billion of reserves. Only $20 billion of that total is cash. The remaining reserves are deposit balances at Federal Reserve Banks. Reserves [created by the Fed] are the base on which the banking system has generated the bulk of the nations money.[20]

Rewriting the above quote to remove the excess verbiage, we have:

> Deposit creation accounts for most of the $375 billion of money. Banks hold only $40 billion of cash which is the base on which the banks generated the bulk of the nations money.

---

19   Exponential growth is very rapid, similar to how rabbits and bacteria reproduce (the population doubles in a given unit of time). Debt grows at the rate $D = P(1+r)^n$ where D = debt at the end of the year; P = principal borrowed; r = interest rate (10% is 0.1); n = number of years. This is the compound interest formula. For an easy to read explanation of exponential growth, see *The Truth in Money Book*, Thoren and Warner, Truth in Money, Inc., 1985, (P.O. Box 30, Chagrin Falls, Ohio, 44022), p. 79-81.

20   *I Bet You Thought*, Federal Reserve Bank of New York, 1984, p. 27. Brackets added.

In other words, the bulk of the nation's money is created by the banks (using bookkeeping), but since banks are in the business of loaning money and not giving it away, this means that the bulk of our money supply is debt that must be paid back. Our currency (which is bookkeeping money converted into cash) is also debt. Furthermore, the $40 billion of cash reserves is not considered part of the money supply because it isn't circulating; this money is used by banks to cash checks on demand, and maintain legal reserve requirements. If any of the $40 billion is put into circulation, this reduces the money supply by the fractional-reserve multiplier; i.e., if a $10 check is cashed, the money supply is reduced by about $100.

Perhaps you are thinking that the money your boss paid you belongs to you; this can't be debt. True, for you it is not a debt, but where did your boss get it; from his customers? Where did they get it? The money you have was originally borrowed from a bank by somebody at sometime, even though it may have changed hands many times. INTEREST MUST BE PAID ON IT.

Unpayable Increasing Debt is Inevitable

Let us set the stage and pretend that we want to create and maintain a constant money supply of $100 billion (B) each year (Figure 2.1). Since most of the money supply is at the same time a debt to the banks, this debt is shown as a separate block.

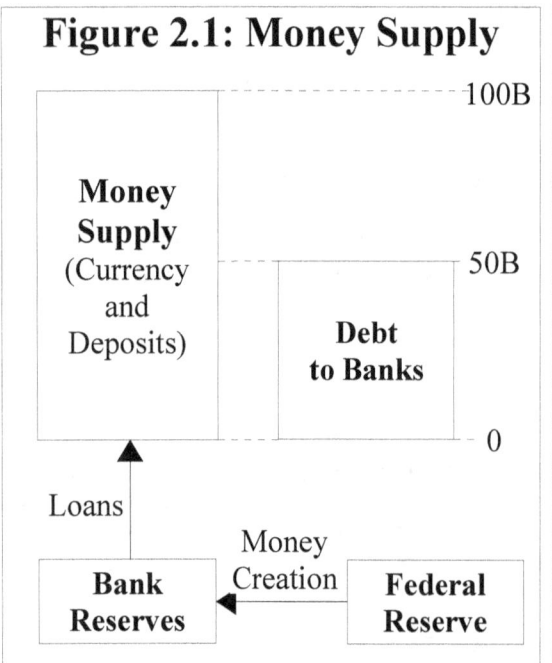

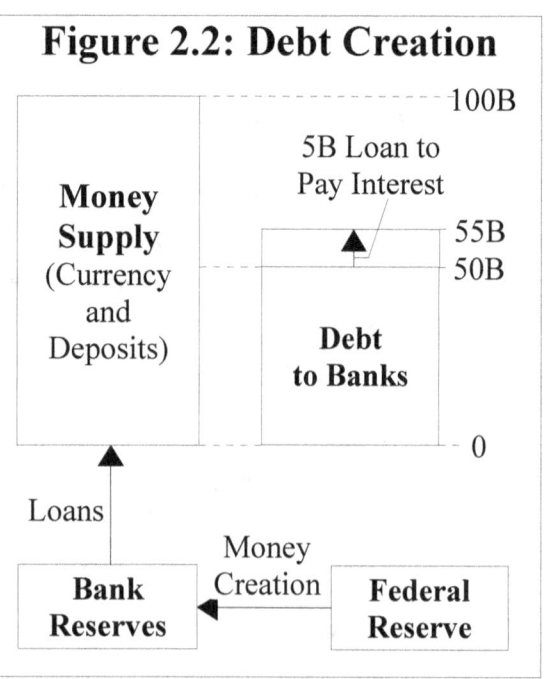

We can start the debt at any amount we want because as you will see it must increase, so let us presume that half the money supply ($50B) was created debt free (we don't care how), and the rest ($50B) is debt to the banks at an interest rate of 10%.

At this stage, the "right" amount of money is in circulation, goods and services are being produced and exchanged, and everyone is happy. AT THE END OF THE FIRST YEAR, INTEREST DUE TO THE BANKS IS 10% OF $50B, OR $5B. PAYING THIS INTEREST REDUCES THE MONEY SUPPLY BY $5B. This shortage of money creates a craving that is satisfied by borrowing more. When the banks loan $5B to make up for the lost $5B, **our debt to the banks increases from $50B to $55B** (Figure 2.2). Did you see it? Did you see the most important point in your understanding of how our monetary system works? Debt was unavoidably created.

Why the Monetary System Has to Crash

If you want to understand why the monetary system *has* to crash[21], you have to understand the point made in the last section, that from one year to the next, debt to the banking system is forced to increase (regardless of whether government balances its budget), and there is nothing in the system to prevent it. Year after year, in order to maintain the money supply at the desired level, debt will increase. Let's see what happens over a period of years:

Next year: The interest due has increased from $5B to $5.5 B. The banks will loan this $5.5B maintaining our desired $100 B money supply. But our total debt will again increase from $55B to $60.5B (55 + 5.5). Figure 2.3 shows how the debt increases exponentially over several years while the money supply remains constant. In year 10 the debt exceeds the money supply; it is now impossible to pay back! Since the debt can never be paid back, it never will be paid back. It will be a permanent debt that continues to grow year after year.

When the point is reached (as it eventually must) in which the interest due on the debt exceeds the total output of the nation, defaults on loans *must* occur, along with bankruptcies. Are you starting to see why you lost your house, why your company went out of business so you lost your job, and why you were forced to consume your savings?

---

21   There is an issue of "sustainability" discussed in Appendix A that will allow the system to last a long time.

Figure 2.3: Charting the Growth of Debt

Year	Money Supply (Billions)	Debt to Banks (Billions)
1	100	50
2	100	55
5	100	73
10	100	118
20	100	306
50	100	5336

Rising Prices

There are two elements to rising prices. First, rising interest payments paid by corporations on their exponentially rising debt are passed on to the consumer as rising prices. As of 1987 about 40% of corporate profits were used to pay interest on their debts. According to *The Spotlight*, Nov. 9 1987 issue, in the article "Market Collapse Inevitable" (p. 1):

> Even so-called conventional debt turned into a stranglehold on productive enterprises, which set aside four cents out of every dollar in operating revenue for debt service in 1962.

> By 1984, Wall Street analysts note, debt obligation jumped more than 10-fold; debt service for the average industrial firm ate up more than 40 cents of every dollar earned.

Second, in order for companies to pay the interest on their debt, banks have to create this money because it doesn't exist, and the Fed must have a liberal monetary policy to allow this money to be created otherwise there will be bankruptcies, and banks will have to write off bad debt. In order for prices to remain stable, this newly created money must be balanced by newly created goods. In other words, national output must increase at a rate that equals or exceeds the interest rate. Typically national output (i.e. GDP) grows at 3% and interest rate is much greater, so the money put into circulation to pay the interest will increase faster than goods, causing prices to rise. To hold back rising prices, the only mechanism available to the Fed is to reduce the money supply, forcing business and bank failures.

Increased Productivity Does Not Reduce Debt

Some students of economics believe that the debt can be paid back or reduced by increasing productivity. I will now show that increased productivity will not reduce debt to the banking system. The only way to reduce debt is to pay it down by reducing the money supply, creating a shortage of money. If you already accept this point, you can skip the following belabored but easy to read section.

Increased productivity can be looked at three ways. First, new companies can be started and funded by the banks (the Fed creates additional reserves to allow the banks to create the additional money to lend). Second, new companies are funded by profits, wages, venture capitalists, or people with money (non-bank sources). And third, producers can produce more for less cost (are more efficient).

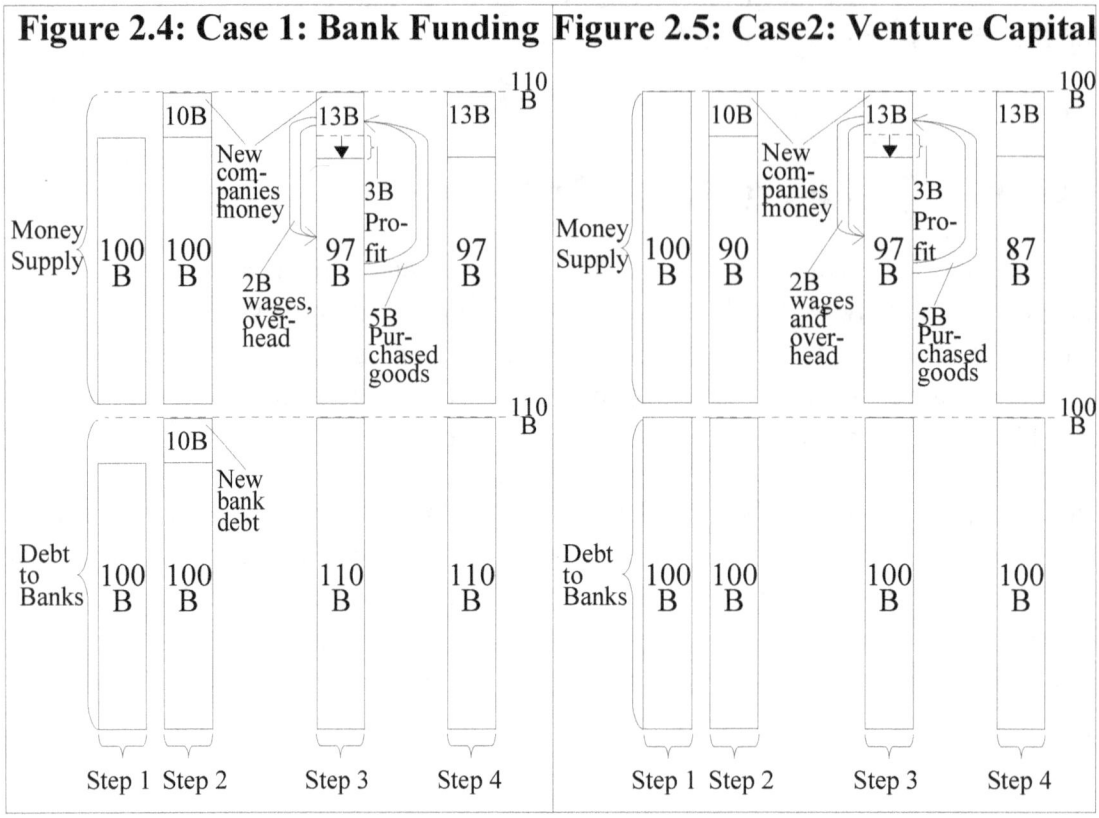

Figure 2.4: Case 1: Bank Funding   **Figure 2.5: Case2: Venture Capital**

Case 1: Increased productivity from new companies funded by banks.

Refer to Figure 2.4. Let's start with an initial money supply of $100 Billion (B) and a level of debt of $100B (Step 1). Next, many new startup companies together borrow $10B from the banks (Step 2); this increases the money supply *and the debt* both by $10B. Both are now $110B. Let us assume we want to maintain the money supply at $110B; this additional money will be balanced by the newly produced goods and services to maintain stable prices. During the first year of operation, the companies produced and sold $5B of goods and spend $2B on wages, overhead, and raw materials (Step 3); this leaves $3B of profit. The result: The money supply and the debt still equal each other (Step 4) even though the companies were productive and made $3B of profit. As you can see, money has circulated, changed hands (Step 3), but the entire process took place *within* the money supply, not external to it. The debt cannot be reduced unless the money supply is reduced to pay it (creating a recession). At the end of the year, 10% interest will be due to the banks on $110B of debt, causing the debt to exceed the money supply.

Case 2: Increased productivity from new companies funded by profits, wages, or venture capitalists, (but not from banks).

Refer to Figure 2.5. Again we start with an initial money supply of $100B and a level of debt of $100B (Step 1). Next, many new startup companies together borrow $10B from venture capitalists, or earn it from wages or sales. The money supply changes hands (the startup companies have more of it now); the debt to the banks remains the same (Step 2). During the first year of operation the companies make $3B in profit as before (Step 3). But look at how the money supply and the debt have changed (Step 4): They haven't!

As in Case 1, productivity caused money to change hands, but the debt cannot be reduced unless the money supply is reduced to pay it. Since there are more goods on the market competing for the same money supply, the result will be a recession. We want increased productivity (more goods) to be balanced with more money.

Case 3: Increased productivity through increased efficiency

Increased efficiency changes the proportion of profit to cost, but does not affect the debt. We can change the amounts in Step 3 (Figures 2.4 or 2.5) to reduce the cost of business ($2B instead of $3B), and increase the profit ($4B instead of $3B). All exchanges occur within the money supply, not external to it. The debt is not affected.

A Look at Debt Free Money

I made a simplifying assumption that no debt-free money is placed into circulation, but in fact some of the money is created debt-free. If enough debt-free money is put into circulation, it can be used to pay the interest to the banks so that debt wouldn't increase.

Coins minted by the Treasury account for about 3% of the money supply. When the Treasury mints coins, the newly minted coins are sold to the Fed who pays face value for the coins. This is debt-free money. Once a sufficient number of coins are put into circulation, the annual input of coins needed to maintain the desired level will be negligible. Since only an ongoing influx of debt-free money can pay the ongoing interest payments, coins do not help significantly.

When gold is mined, the Treasury buys the gold and transfers title of it to the Fed by selling them Gold Certificates. This is debt-free money, but it only amounts to perhaps $1 billion per year.[22] This is insignificant when compared to $150 B in interest on the national debt.

Of course, the government does not create money to pay its bills (that's a myth); it either collects taxes, or borrows. There is no significant ongoing debt free money to prevent debt from increasing.

Why You Can't Save

The public policy of our government is that you should save your money, because when you put it in the bank, the bank can use it to make business loans. You are rewarded by being paid interest. Unfortunately, mathematics works against government policy, making it very hard to save.

Since it is reasonable for a nation to have savings, let's consider the consequences if 50 million Americans decided to save $10,000 in the bank, a total of $500 billion at interest. After the first year they will be paid 6% after-tax interest of $30 billion (assuming an interest rate in "normal" times). In the 40th year they will get $309 billion in interest. In the 80th year, they will receive $3.2 trillion, a large portion of the nation's output. In any given year, each person will get paid his interest. No year is any different from any other, so if the people get paid $30 billion interest in the first year, they will get paid $3.2 trillion interest in the 80th, guaranteed by the FDIC and government. To allow Americans to save $10,000 at compound interest, would within a few decades bankrupt the nation. This is why immense system pressures work to prevent Americans from saving their money.

These pressures include: Rising prices (interest earnings loses most of its value); Bankruptcies (savings are taken from you); Unemployment (forces you to spend your savings); Business cycle and recession (forces bankruptcies and unemployment); Welfare (pays the unemployed; can't let you starve); Inheritance tax and end-of-life medical bills (takes away a lifetime of interest earnings); War, the welfare state, heavy property, income, and sales taxes (takes your money so you can't save); etc. That Americans cannot save is confirmed by statistics. The average American, if he cashed out all his assets and paid off his liabilities, would either own nothing, or be in debt to the system.[23]

---

22 See http://minerals.er.usgs.gov/minerals/pubs/commodity/gold/mcs-2011-gold.pdf for domestic production of gold from 2006 – 2010.

While Americans on the average cannot save, this does not mean that individuals cannot save. If a small number such as 10,000 people deposit $10 million into a bank at 6% interest, in 80 years their money will multiply by 100 times to $10 trillion. Interest paid on $10 trillion is $600 billion, roughly equivalent to federal income taxes. This is how the wealthy class produces nothing and lives off of the producers. Usury is a large hidden tax. How do you pay this hidden tax? As stated previously, interest costs to businesses are passed on to consumers in the form of rising prices. In 1962, interest was only 4% of corporate operating revenue; by 1984 it exceeded 40%.

Isn't it the American dream to deposit $10,000 in the bank when we are 25, and retire at age 65 when our money grows to $100,000? Did you not consider that if you worked for the first $10,000, nine other people had to work to give you the other $90,000? Isn't this theft? While money is superior to barter, it has limitations that must be understood. The purpose of money is to exchange wealth, not create it without productivity.

The prohibition of usury would, until recently, have been considered outlandish, but now that we are in the grip of global depression and bankruptcies, true solutions are needed. Islamic bankers do not practice usury, but invest money instead. Investment means you are a part owner.[24] You share in the risk and the profits, and you are paid on the basis of *productivity*. Interest means you get paid on the basis of *time*, whether or not anything is produced, and there is no risk (guaranteed by the FDIC). Alternate systems do exist and do work.

The net effect is that you will find it difficult to save money in a monetary system that pays interest, and the money you do make from the productive efforts of others through interest on your savings will be taken from you by indirect means.

---

23   A study by the Federal Reserve Board of all financial assets held by individuals (excluding what was held by institutions), and calculating their net financial worth (assets minus debts) reported the following:
"... 54 percent of the total net financial assets were held by the 2 percent of families with the greatest amount of such assets and 86 percent by the top 10 percent; 55 percent of the families in the sample had zero or negative net worth." *Secrets of the Temple*, William Greider, Simon and Schuster, 1987, p. 39

24   See http://en.wikipedia.org/wiki/Islamic_banking.

Are You Sure There Is a Problem?

It is surprising that there are people who actually believe that our monetary system works. Given the fact that our money is created as debt, I find it hard to draw any conclusion other than that it doesn't work. There are others who share my position. Robert H. Hemphill, former Credit Manager of the Federal Reserve Bank of Atlanta said:

> If all the bank loans were paid, no one would have a bank deposit, and there would not be a dollar of coin or currency in circulation. This is a staggering thought. We are completely dependent on the commercial banks. Someone has to borrow every dollar we have in circulation, cash or credit. If the banks create ample synthetic money, we are prosperous; if not, we starve. We are absolutely without a permanent monetary system. When one gets a complete grasp upon the picture, the tragic absurdity of our hopeless position is almost incredible— but there it is. It (the banking problem) is the most important subject intelligent persons can investigate and reflect upon. It is so important that our present civilization may collapse unless it is widely understood and the defects remedied very soon.[25]

Robert L. Owen brings into question whose side the Fed is really on:

> It should be perfectly obvious that the mandate in the [Federal Reserve] act that the powers of the System should be employed to accommodate commerce and industry has been entirely ignored by the Federal Reserve Board, and the Board of Governors of the Federal Reserve System, for they have pursued policies resulting in and permitting the absolute destruction of both commerce and industry in the past, as pointed out in the evidence taken on the Patman bill in the testimony of the author of this book, as well as by the testimony of others.[26]

In the next chapter we will look at solutions. You will be surprised at what I propose, because most people think my solution is the very cause of the problem! I propose that the Government pay its bills by merely creating the money to pay them; then the debt could be reduced. "But that's inflationary!" you say. Is it really?

---

25 This is quoted by a lot of authors, but I could not find the original source for this quote.
26 Robert L. Owen, former Chairman, Committee on Banking and Currency, *National Economy and the Banking System*, Senate Document No. 23, 76th Congress 1st session, Presented by Mr. Logan Jan 24, 1939, p. 102. Many good quotes on pages 98-104. This is a good book on economics.

Chapter 3

A Monetary System Free From

Unpayable Debt and Taxes

In the first two chapters we learned how our money supply, created and loaned into circulation by the banking system, creates unpayable debt that is responsible for virtually all our economic problems.

In this chapter, we will look at a way to structure a monetary system capable of supporting unbridled prosperity and heaven on earth. What a blessing for society. Yes, even income tax can be done away with. Read on...

Debt-Free Money: The Basis of an Ideal System

We learned in the first two chapters that in today's unpayable debt-based monetary system, virtually all the money in circulation is debt that must be paid back plus interest. As seen in Figure 3.1, the banks create and loan the money into circulation; this process of converting debt into money is called "monetizing debt." It is removed from circulation by repaying the principal; the interest increases the unpayable debt.

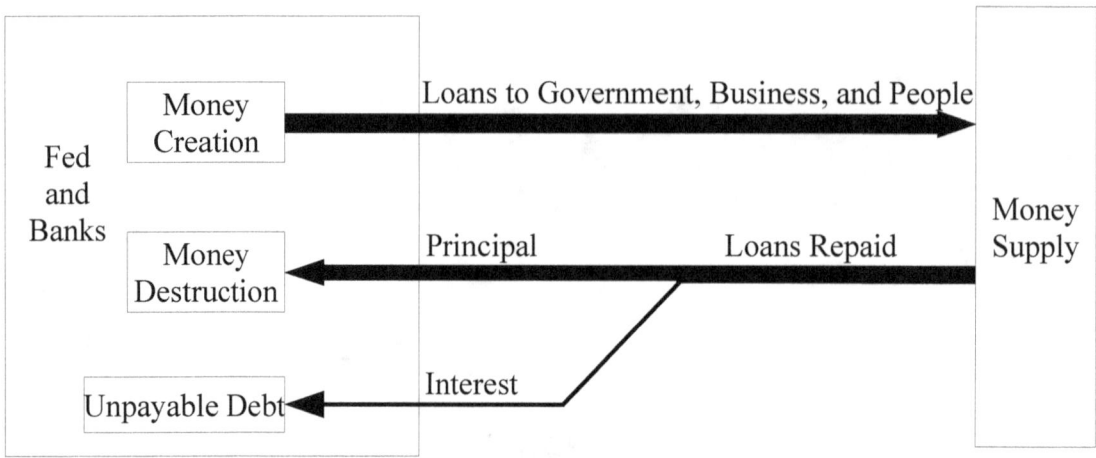

Figure 3.1: Our Unpayable-Debt Based Monetary System

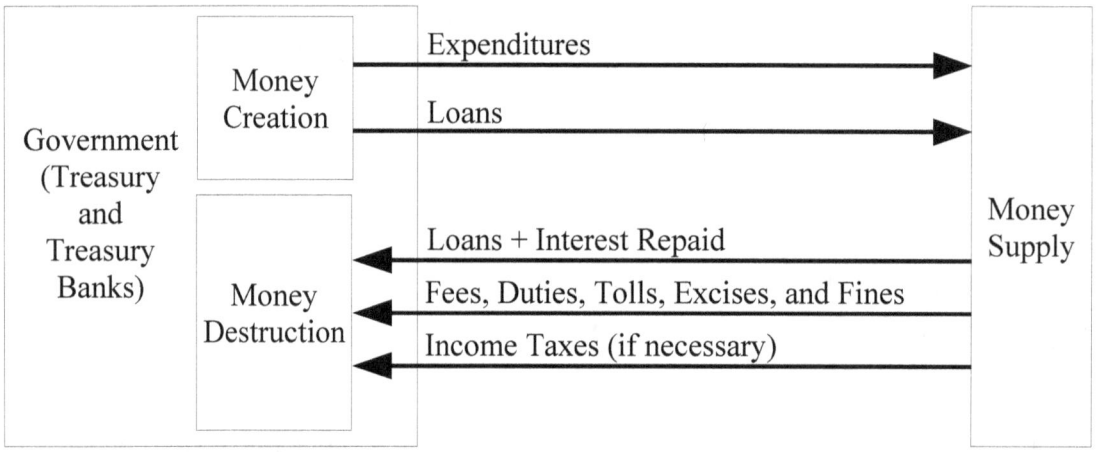

Figure 3.2: A Balanced Monetary System

Debt is a design defect because only the principal is created, never the interest. ***The interest payments demanded in law do not exist in actuality***, so the difference is made up by creating unpayable debt. Figures 3.1 and 3.2 are the most important part of this book because they provide, in graphical and simple form, the problem and the solution to monetary system design.

Furthermore, the often but wrongly stated purpose of interest is to compensate the owner of money for the time he no longer has use of it.[27] Since a money supply is

---

27   I disagree that the owner of money should be paid for the time he no longer has use of it. They are a string of words without substance. The concept looks good until you look at the effect it has on society. Buying into this concept costs the nation half a trillion dollars a year. The purpose of money is to facilitate exchange, not to make money without producing anything for it.

permanent, it has no time-value, and there is no reason that banks should loan it into circulation and make money on it.

In a balanced system, Government will take back its Constitutional power to create money that was delegated to the Federal Reserve.[28] It would consist of debt free money (never has to be paid back) plus loans at interest that benefit the nation by reducing or eliminating taxes. As seen in Figure 3.2, the Government (Treasury) creates, spends, and loans the money into circulation.

To maintain stable prices, money is removed from circulation by interest on loans, fees, duties, tolls, excises, fines, and only if necessary, direct taxes and personal income taxes.[29]

How to Have No Price Inflation <u>And</u> No Recession (Plenty of Money)

Today's price inflation is not caused by too much money; it is caused by rising interest payments on the rising debt, which are passed on to the consumer. Since there is no inherent mechanism for reducing debt (Figure 3.1), the Fed will suppress rising prices by maintaining a shortage of money in circulation. This creates a craving for money, in the midst of abundance on market's shelves.

In the unpayable-debt free based system shown in Figure 3.2, the money supply can be increased through expenditures, or decreased through fees, etc. This makes it possible to adjust the money supply independently, without affecting business funding, resulting in price stability without recession.

---

28   Article 1, Section 8, Clause 5 of the Constitution states: "The Congress shall have the power ... to coin money [and] regulate the value thereof...". I read a court opinion, now lost to me, that held that the coining of money meant the stamping of metal.

29   A direct tax is a tax upon property for no other reason than that you own it. An indirect tax is a tax on the use of the property. Since the time of the U.S. Constitution, it was expected that State funding would be provided by direct taxes; the Federal government would use direct taxes only in emergencies, and it would have to be apportioned amongst the several states. I personally don't like direct taxes; if we are to have the right to property, direct taxes upon property needs to be done away with. If you don't pay the tax, it is seized and sold to pay the tax due.

The U.S. Supreme Court said: "[The] original expectation was that the power of direct taxation would be exercised only in extraordinary exigencies, and down to August 15, 1894, this expectation has been realized." *Pollock v. Farmers' Loan & Trust*, 157 U.S. 429, 574 (1895).

In an unpayable-debt based system, the amount of money in circulation depends on the amount of loans the banks make. If prices start to rise, the Fed will reduce the money supply and/or raise interest rates, which reduces the loans to the nation. This makes business funding more expensive, while at the same time slows economic activity resulting in lower profits and recession.

In an unpayable-debt free system in which the banks are nationalized, **control of price level by change in the money supply, is independent of business funds availability**. Businesses are funded on the basis of demand, and price level **has no bearing** on interest rates or fund availability for businesses. If more businesses demand money, that does not make the money scarcer or more expensive. All businesses are accommodated at a nominal interest rate.[30] The increase in business funds will give rise to increased goods and services which will sooner or later create balance without requiring a change in the money supply. If prices start to rise, the money supply is reduced, but businesses will never feel it because loans availability and interest rate are not controlled or affected by money supply.

Loaning Money Transfers Title of the Money Supply to the Lenders

There is a "truth in money" movement that advocates that the ultimate solution to our economic problems is to have the government create money and spend it into circulation to pay its bills.

Absolutely, any solution must include debt-free money, but this is not enough. Even if we begin with a totally debt-free system, *if private banks (or entities) are permitted to make loans at interest, they will gain title to the money supply, and thereby the entire wealth of the nation*. This may explain how 1% of the nation's population acquired 36% of the wealth, and how 10% of the population acquired 86% of the wealth. The average American either has no financial wealth, or is in debt to the system.[31]

---

30 When I was a kid in the 1960s, I recall that some senator (Kennedy?) promoted wage and price controls because interest rates exceeded an ungodly 3%. I think 3% or less is not an excessive rate to charge businesses. Consider that credit cards charge merchants around 2.5%. But then, I could be caught in an illusion; 3% may be ungodly high.

31 A study by the Federal Reserve Board of all financial assets held by individuals (excluding what was held by institutions), and calculating their net financial worth (assets minus debts) reported the following:

Imagine a small nation with a debt-free money supply of $1 Billion (B). An engineer decides to save $1,000 a year. In 10 years he has socked away $10,000; in 20 years $20,000. At this rate, in 1 million years he will end up owning the entire $1B money supply. One million years is so long, no society need fear this man's actions.

Now imagine a banker who loans $1,000 at 10% annual interest. In the first year he is repaid $1,100 which he then relends. Year after year, the money is repaid and immediately loaned out again. In just 145 years, he ends up owning the entire $1B money supply. All of it is still in circulation, but he gets to decide who will have it and who will not.

How has the banker been so much more productive to society than the engineer, that he should end up owning the entire money supply? The answer is he hasn't; he has merely taken advantage of the **exponential** rate of growth from loaning money at compound interest, which is far more rapid (145 years) than natural forms of increase.

To allow anyone to engage in the profession of loaning money at interest is to allow him to end up owning everything. Furthermore, if *you* deposit $1,000 in a bank at 10% compound interest, the same result occurs. In 145 years, you will be a billionaire. If 1,000 people do the same thing, then somehow $1 trillion in wealth is suppose to be created *without any productivity*. Obviously, this system can't work.

The problem can be solved by either requiring banks to *invest* money (no paying or charging of interest), or by nationalizing the banks, making them part of the Treasury, or making them part of state or local governments, but in any case taking them out of private hands.[32] When government loans money the interest is removed from circulation, and compounding wouldn't occur. The concept of compounding or exponential growth has no meaning to an agency that can create and destroy money at will. And interest would reduce the tax load. Placing the banks into public hands does not mean that bank personnel will lose their jobs, they just become government employees. It means that no one will be allowed to gain title to the money supply.

I am of the opinion that interest charged by private entities must be prohibited, or compounding will occur, regardless of the interest rate. What gives rise to compounding is the **buying and selling** of money. That means that if we want to continue with the

---

... 54 percent of the total net financial assets were held by the 2 percent of families with the greatest amount of such assets and 86 percent by the top 10 percent; 55 percent of the families in the sample had zero or negative net worth. *Secrets of the Temple,* William Greider, Simon and Schuster, 1987, p. 39.

32   The banks can be purchased from the owners at a fair market value, through the legal process of eminent domain; the money for the transaction is created by government.

loan system that we have today, the banks will have to be nationalized. Money is a public utility and should be treated as such. If we are unwilling to nationalize the banks, then we must find alternatives.[33]

Some will argue that you can't trust government and political control with something so important as money, that private ownership will more likely secure stability and honesty. Putting trust aside, the *properties* are different. Interest to private banks is compounded until the bankers own everything. Interest to treasury banks is destroyed; there is no compounding, no increase in debt, and less taxes.

On the question of trust, would you rather trust a banker for a $50,000 mortgage and pay $150,000 in interest, or pay a treasury bank $10,000 in administrative fees for the same $50,000? Would you rather the nation pay several hundred billion of annual interest on the money supply, or pay nothing to the treasury? Who would you trust more to keep us out of war: banks who profit from government borrowing money for weapons, or the treasury which does not profit from war?

What is Usury?

Usury (i.e., a fee paid for the *use* of money) means the charging of interest at any rate, as well as charging a fee for the use of money.[34] The modern meaning of usury is the practice of charging excessive, unreasonably high, and often illegal interest rates on loans. We can list some of its properties that make it prohibited. Usury is the making of money simply by having money and not taking any risk or doing any work or making any effort. Usury is there when unpayable debt is created (there is more debt than there is money in circulation to pay it back), or when compounding of money occurs.

We Can Have an Income Tax-Free System If We Want It

In the present system, taxes are used to fund government expenditures. In an unpayable-debt free system, taxes are used to remove money from circulation, not to fund expenditures which are freely available by simply creating and spending it into

---

33 See http://en.wikipedia.org/wiki/Islamic_banking for alternative practices.
34 http://en.wikipedia.org/wiki/Usury. Read the links to other pages. For a history of usury, see www.monetary.org/interest.htm.

circulation. Of course, overall the amount of money that can be created is based on maintaining stable price levels.

In an unpayable-debt free system, government expenditures are created and spent into circulation (Figure 3.2), and an equal amount must somehow be removed from circulation, otherwise the money supply will increase and prices will rise (unless the increase is balanced by increased goods and services).

Fees, duties, excises, tolls, and imposts will remove money from circulation. If this is not enough to provide a personal income tax free system, there are other methods of removing the money from circulation that has been spent into circulation. Prior to the creation of the welfare state and the numerous social agencies in 1933, there was no need for personal income tax. The U.S. Supreme Court stated in 1895:

> Until the past few years, the United States has generally been able to obtain all needful revenue from the single source of duties upon imports."[35]

If banks belonged to the U.S. Treasury, then profits from the banks would be removed from circulation, and this money might be great enough that it would remove the need for personal income taxes. If we want a tax free society, it is not impossible, we only have to choose it.

Funding for the General Welfare

I have a strong objection to government taxing and spending for the general welfare which amounts to give-away programs for special interests,[36] and the buying of votes. I do not believe in general welfare as propounded by one major political party; I think it is a violation of natural law because funding comes from taxes which are mandatory and for such purposes tantamount to stealing.

---

35 *Pollock v. Farmers' Loan & Trust*, 157 U.S. 429, 623 (1895); quoting Pomeroy's Constitutional Law (Sec 281); no date.

36 Funding for medicine is not at all general welfare to those who spend money to avoid getting sick. Those who do not subscribe to the government and medical establishment's paradigm of drugs and doctors, cannot partake of the funding. Government will not pay for high quality organic non-GMO food and food supplements, only for expensive drugs. If it is not a general welfare, it should not be done by government. Furthermore, funding for research to find cures for cancer and diabetes will pour money down a rats hole. Why would the medical establishment want to find a cure for their $multi-billion profit centers? The cures are already available to those who would care to look; I personally know of 6 cures for cancer; see Hidden-Cancer-Cures.com, and Hidden-Diabetes-Cures.com. The same applies to the educational establishment. When 1 in 5 high school graduates in the US cannot read their diploma (www.stateline.org/live/details/speech?contentId=16052), this is a sign that these people should be defunded; make them compete.

Alternative Transactions

Here are some examples of alternatives to our current debt-based system.

Home Purchase: Today a buyer may pay $200,000 for a $50,000 house; $150,000 goes to the bank to pay interest. There is no risk to the bank because the house is the collateral for the loan. If the owner can't make payments on the mortgage,[37] the bank can foreclose and auction the house at a price that will recover the bank's money but not the buyer's money - and the buyer loses everything.

As an alternative, the treasury bank would buy the $50,000 house, and sell it to the buyer for (say) $60,000 with payments spread over so many years. The $10,000 profit would be in the nature of a service charge or tax.[38] How can a buyer guarantee that he can unconditionally make payments each month for 30 years? If the house has to be sold, the proceeds could be split according to equity. This would motivate the treasury bank to sell it for the highest price, not just the price that will recover its cost. The buyer would agree to make repairs and allow regular inspections in order to protect the community from loss. And, payments can be structured based on a percentage of take-home pay. If the economy is in a recession and the buyer is laid off, payments can cease. Whereas a bank is in the business to make money, the treasury does not lose anything by waiting. There may need to be a time limit to prevent abuse, but these are details to be worked out. This would eliminate the unfairness of mortgages.

Business Funding: In the current debt-based system, a loan is paid back at a rate based on *time*. If productivity is at a standstill or the economy goes into a recession, the company is at risk because interest must still be paid even though little is being produced.

In a usury free system, a bank would provide a loan whose interest rate is based on the company's own rate of return. Assuming monthly payments to the bank, both principal and interest would have a floating rate. The more the company produces, the greater is the profit of the bank. If the company fails, the bank gets nothing. Thus, the

---

37 A mortgage is when you sell your property (typically to a bank), and you have equitable right of recovery provided you don't miss any payments. If you miss a payment, the bank can foreclose, which means you lose the right of recovery.

38 For those who promote private banks, even if a private bank accepted the reduction in profit from $150,000 to $10,000, nevertheless compounding is still occurring, though at a lower effective interest rate. They loan $50,000 and get $60,000 back. They reloan the $60,000 and get $72,000 back... (I am ignoring business expenses, which lower the effective interest rate). Compounding; it is why I am dead set against private banks. If you want a system that will facilitate heaven on earth, boot the private banks. There is nothing they can do that a public bank cannot do.

bank shares in the risk as well as the profit of the business. This loan is paid back at a rate based on the natural rate of *productivity,* and is a floating interest rate. Once the loan is repaid, the profit sharing is concluded.[39]

With venture capital, in an equity-based system, a bank or venture capitalist provides the financing while the entrepreneur provides the labor. Both share in the profits and the risk.[40]

Municipal Funding: Today, if city (or state) governments need money to build a bridge, they borrow the money by issuing bonds. The interest on the bonds can triple the cost of the bridge.

In an interest-free system, the federal treasury gives money to the cities for stated purposes. As part of the funding, the city submits a plan for removing the excess money from circulation. The city is required to employ some alternate means (including possibly collecting taxes) if the submitted plan doesn't work out and prices rise. However, the improvement in infrastructure may increase the goods and services produced, precluding the need to remove the money.

Prices can be monitored regionally, and every region can increase or decrease the money supply as necessary to bring price levels into line with national averages. This will prevent the occurrence of depressions in some areas while booms are occurring in others.

Another possibility is for the federal government to give municipalities, on demand, an intentionally depreciating currency which would coexist alongside of the stable currency issued by the federal government. Originally I thought that a depreciating currency was the stupidest idea I ever heard of, but changed my mind. A depreciating currency might lose ½ or 1% of its value per month, which would automatically take the money out of circulation. Because no one wants to hold on to it for long, it will force a huge circulation, promoting trade and prosperity in the community. These local currencies would be branded by local communities (whether state, county, or city level), and generally accepted by local merchants promoting local

---

39 A floating interest rate, based on the productivity of the business, is not usury because the return to the bank is not guaranteed on the basis of time which may be impossible, and the bank shares in the risk. Collateral for the loan would remove the risk to the bank, making the loan usurious. A key point is that the return to the bank is linked to the natural return of Nature, and not an artificial gain impossible to achieve.

40 Some argue that those who invest their money in companies are making money without producing anything. I believe that they are in fact a part owner in the company and share in the risk. If the company fails, they lose their money. It is the element of *risk* that distinguishes usury from investment. Loans are generally collateralized so that the banker takes no risk.

commerce, though the city, state, or county government may only accept the currency they issued, for payment of taxes. This will tend to restrict its use to the local area, as it is the acceptance for payment of taxes that gives it its value.[41]

Summary Points for a Monetary System that will Support Heaven on Earth

1) The Government never borrows, but creates money and spends it into circulation to pay its bills.

2) To maintain stable prices, new money put into circulation is balanced by new goods and services put into circulation, or by money taken out of circulation. Rising prices are controlled by taking action to decrease the money supply, and falling prices are controlled by taking action to increase the money supply.

3) To prevent the creation of unpayable debt, and to keep the money supply free, a sufficient quantity of money is placed into circulation debt-free.

4) To prevent recession, business funding is available on demand, and availability is not linked to money supply or price-level controls. When business funding is unhindered, this will produce a natural maximum employment; there will be no need to try to reduce unemployment.

5) To prevent anyone from gaining title to the money supply, creating and/or loaning of the nation's money at interest is not permitted to individuals, private banks, or non-government entities; only Treasury banks are permitted.[42]

6) For the benefit of society, there are no personal income taxes.

7) Control of the money supply is placed into the hands of engineers who are intimately familiar with the theory and practice of control system design.[43] The goal of the control system is price stability, while making money freely available to the nation.

---

41   The Guernsey Experiment, the Wara currency, the Woergl currency (which depreciates), and the Palma currency are examples of local currencies. See http://fairfieldhotpotato.com/SuccessStories.html.

42   Non-nations money such as barter script is still permissible. Individuals should be able to make loans to family members or friends, as long as it is not a business or otherwise abusive.

43   Economists have shown their inability to manage the public purse.

The designer of a monetary system should ask one fundamental question: "Can anyone make money off of the system without being productive?" Any such feature should be designed out of the system or made illegal, as the purpose of money is to *exchange* productivity.

The First Step: Tax the Fed

To get people comfortable with debt-free money, the first step might be to *tax the Fed* for something as minor as balancing the budget. Congress may be unwilling to tax their constituency to make up the budget shortfall, but they might be willing to tax the Fed. It does not require changing any relationships or nationalizing anything. People can see the effect of debt-free money. It would have to be done carefully because you can expect the "powers that be" to make it look bad.

The Fed would create the money by bookkeeping entry, crediting the Treasury's account. This debt-free money, spent into circulation by the Government, would make it possible to start to pay the previously unpayable debt owed to the banks.

The next step might be to redeem all interest bearing Government debt instruments. Since the government will be creating its own money (via taxing the Fed), it no longer needs to borrow, and it has as much money as it wants to redeem its securities. The national debt must be done away with, and the easiest way is to create the money to pay it off. Then start paying for infrastructure repairs, gradually taking bigger steps.

As the debts to the banks are paid, interest payments will be reduced, and prices will fall as companies pass the savings on to consumers. To prevent price inflation due to excess money in circulation, the reserve requirement will be raised so that the new money becomes bank reserves and can't be put into circulation. This new money will then have the sole effect of paying off bank debt; the money supply will remain unchanged.

The next step might be to nationalize the Fed. And finally, a time has to come when either banks are prohibited from making loans, or banks are nationalized.

Chapter 4

What is Money?

Up to now I have relied on your intuition about what money is. It is an important question, and now is the time to go back and fill in that detail.

The definition of money will tell you what it is used for, its various properties, and distinguish it from other similar items or concepts. Money can take many forms; some will produce peace and unbridled prosperity in society, others will produce war, slavery, and universal poverty. This makes it vitally important that people understand what characteristics are necessary of a monetary system to achieve our goal of creating heaven on earth.

Definition

Money is that which is used as a medium of exchange by a community. In order to be accepted as such, the media must have value. Money has a known value, against which the value of all commodities can be measured.

Money is distinguished from barter in that barter is the exchange of one or more commodities directly for another. The commodities involved are not money because they are not generally accepted by the community for trade, and they are not a basis upon which all other commodities value can be compared.

Anything can be placed into circulation to act as money, as long as the item has value, doesn't wear out or rot, and can't be counterfeited. That value might be due to its intrinsic commodity value, or its natural scarcity, or man-made scarcity, or its acceptance by government in payment of taxes, or other means.

Different Forms of Money and their Properties

Many things can and have been used as money, and each has its own peculiar properties, advantages, and disadvantages. Some things used as money are nevertheless not suitable for use as money because of the problems they cause, but they are by the above definition still money.

A useful property for money is that it be a store of wealth, which requires that it maintain a fixed constant value, though historically societies have been plundered by not maintaining the value of their money. Some designs for money might have its value decrease with time in order to motivate people to circulate it, but then it is not useful as a store of wealth.

Money may be embodied in a commodity such as gold or silver metal by weight, and may be made into coins or bars stamped with the weight. The coin would not say "One Dollar," but would say "One Ounce." The value of this money will change as the market for the commodity changes, and thus it is not very good in fulfilling the purpose of money to measure the value of all commodities; i.e., if prices rise, it could mean that the value of the gold has fallen. There is nothing sacred about gold and silver to make them an absolute reference for value. Prices of all commodities will rise and fall as the market for these money-commodities rises and falls. People who own large quantities of the commodity can reap huge profits if they can control price levels. Contracts based on the value of money today will incur an unfair loss to someone tomorrow when the value of the money changes. Also, the property of money as a store of wealth is lost when the value of the savings fluctuates from the change in value of the commodity.

Money may be embodied in a commodity such as gold or silver coin, stamped by government into various denominations of the currency of the realm, e.g. "One Dollar," but not "One Ounce." This is a step towards abstraction which allows the government to define the value of the dollar as so many ounces of gold (or silver etc.). A problem with this system is that the value of the commodity (gold in this case) can increase as it becomes more scarce, while the defined value of the dollar remains the same. If the value of the metal exceeds the face value of the coin, the coin loses its property of having a known value against which all other commodities can be measured. A $10 coin with $15 of metal will not be circulated at $10. It will be hoarded, or melted down or sold for $15 of goods. Such coinage can keep its face value only if the face value is greater than or equal to the metal value. If the face value is greater than the metal value, the coin is a token whose value is based on law or custom.

If gold is the sole medium of exchange, the money supply cannot be increased; it is fixed by the available supply of gold. If the economy needs more money, too bad. For this reason, while gold can make a monetary system free from price inflation because it is scarce, you cannot create unbridled prosperity from scarcity.

Some will argue that gold is the solution to the monetary problems we are facing. When the problem is usury, the solution to the problem is to outlaw usury; converting to gold without first outlawing usury will only muddy the problem, but you will feel better about it. Money is a creature of law. If the law is corrupt in that it allows usury, we will not be able to keep a gold based system; we were forced off of gold backing in 1971 when President Nixon closed the gold window.

Use of gold and silver coin (bimetallism) will have a problem with the different gold/silver ratios assigned by different nations. By exporting large quantities of gold or silver, one can make money from the slight differences in the official values between countries. This is called arbitrage. Whether the ratio favors gold or silver doesn't matter; the difference in values will create purchasing power. The less valuable one will leave the country to buy the more valuable one, stripping the country of the less valuable currency.

Money may be embodied as paper backed by gold (or silver or other commodity).[44] Every dollar issued in paper could be backed by its equivalent value of gold. If the community needed more money, the government could simply print the paper and use it to buy gold on the open market, for use as backing. Buying the gold would put the paper into circulation to accommodate the community's needs, and simultaneously

---

44   This assumes there is enough gold in existence. According to Robert Owen, the use of gold for currency would not meet our needs:
    In 1929, the volume of this check money rose to $1,230,000,000,000, which at that time was 100 times the total monetary gold supply of the entire world and about 300 times the entire monetary gold supply in the United States.
    It is perfectly obvious that this turn-over of money through checks could not possibly have been supplied by the use of gold. The modern banking system has therefore created conditions which make the use of gold as money entirely impracticable. The use of gold for currency would prevent the huge business which is now being carried on by the American people. [*National Economy and the Banking System*, Senate Document #23, 1939,p. 3.]

purchase its backing. If there is too much paper in circulation, it can be redeemed out of circulation by selling gold.

The government can run the printing press without a problem to buy gold on the open market, because one form on money (paper) is simply being converted into another form (gold); the gold is held as backing to redeem the paper on demand.

If government backs ten dollars of paper currency with, say, one dollar of gold in order to increase the money supply (10% reserve), this is not a good approach, it isn't safe – it opens the door to a run on the banks, and you can bank on it happening. A ten percent reserve will eventually become 1 percent due to society's need for money, and finally we will be forced off gold backing. You cannot unconditionally promise to redeem ten dollars of paper money with only one dollar of gold.

Money may be embodied as paper, wood, or coins of base metal etc. stamped with a larger value. The intrinsic material value is less than its assigned or stamped value; the coins are called "tokens." Provided its value is set a lot higher than the value of the metal of the coin, its value would be independent of the fluctuating market value of the metal. The value would not be controlled by those who owned large amounts of the metal.

Paper[45] money falls in this category and has value by "fiat" (i.e. decree) and is based solely on law, a very abstract form of money which makes it capable of being the best as well as the worst form of money, all dependent on law. It is capable of maintaining constant value, a store of wealth, it can be debt-free and permanent; it can also be the opposite (what we have now). For fiat money to work, the community must have a legal system capable of protecting the value of the money so that prices remain stable. A lawful fiat money can increase according to the needs of the community. The tally stick is an example of an early fiat currency made from wood, issued by King Henry I around 1100 AD, that was protected from counterfeiting and lasted for about 726 years.[46]

Our money (federal reserve notes), is strictly speaking not fiat currency because it is not issued or controlled by government fiat (i.e. decree), but by the private Federal Reserve system. Do not confuse a debt-based currency and its inherent problems, with a fiat currency which, when properly designed, is capable of supporting heaven on earth.

---

45   Anything that has a natural or intentional scarcity can be circulated, as long as it's material is stable, is not easily counterfeited, and protected by law.

46   See http://www.nationalarchives.gov.uk/museum/item.asp?item_id=6 and http://www.larry-adams.com/200509_article.htm.

Some would argue that this embodiment opens the door to abuse by allowing government to inflate the money supply until it becomes worthless.[47] No; it opens the door to the ideal, and I endorse it. Any system can be abused, it all depends on the legal system. What we have now is abuse.

<u>Money may be embodied by bookkeeping entries or computer records</u>, but this is just bookkeeping which mirrors the underlying system, recording how much money is in your account. A community could have a totally cashless computer based money supply that could be based on a commodity, or unpayable-debt, or be debt free.

<u>Money may be embodied as debt</u>. When *banks* loan money, whether a multiple of the money they have, whether gold, paper, or other debt instrument, or bookkeeping entries, the money is embodied as debt. This is known as a debt-money system. It creates unpayable debt, and allows the banks, through compounding, to gain title to the money supply. A debt-money system is a money-pump, pumping (stealing) the money away from society and placing it into the hands of the bankers. It keeps people, business, and governments on the brink of bankruptcy, struggling to make ends meet; it promotes universal poverty and will put any nation into a state of slavery.

Note that it doesn't matter what the reserve requirement is. Fractional reserves or 100% reserves will have the problem of unpayable debt; and whatever the interest rate, the banks will compound their profits to astronomical amounts, though higher rates go faster.

<u>Money may be embodied as instruments of debt issued by individual banks</u>. In the 1800s notes from many different banks were circulated as money, but you had to contend with the question of solvency of each bank and legitimacy of the note. If the bank failed, you lost your money. And you have a debt-money system again. Federal Reserve Notes fall in this category, though they are not legally notes because they are not redeemable in anything (unless you want to redeem a ten for two fives).

<u>Money may be embodied as stocks</u> which represents a share in a company, which has value and can be used as money. However, the changing value of the stock makes it a poor medium of exchange against which the price of all other commodities can be measured. Stocks are often used as money to buy other companies.

---

47   Stephen Zarlenga, founder of the American Monetary Institute, argues that government issued money has a better history of stability than privately issued money. The bankers have won the propaganda war. www.monetary.org

Money may be embodied as checks, money orders, and travelers checks. These are somewhat different in that an endorsement is usually required, but they can be made out to bearer (or the payee left blank) and circulated. You may have had the experience of paying for something with a second-party check that someone made out to you.

When You Pay With Debt Money, Who Owns the Property?

The use of an instrument of debt to buy something creates a legal contortion. When you buy something, you do not own it until you pay for it. Paying for something with a promissory note does not pay for the object. A promise to pay is not the payment. In this regard there is a legal distinction between a Susan B. Anthony coin dollar, and a Federal Reserve Note dollar. The Anthony dollar, not being a promise to pay but the payment, will deliver ownership free and clear; a note can be challenged. For ordinary purposes it makes no difference, but the law has ambiguity, and clever people might attack your car or your house. As stated in *Stanek vs. White,* 215 NW 784, (1927):

> There is a distinction between a debt discharged and one paid. When discharged, the debt still exists, though divested of its character as a legal obligation during the operation of the discharge. Something of the original vitality of the debt continues to exist, which may be transferred even though the transferee takes it subject to the disability incident to the discharge. The fact that it carries something which may be a consideration for a new promise to pay, so as to make an otherwise worthless promise a legal obligation, makes it the subject of transfer by assignment.

The use of Federal Reserve Notes creates legal contortions, and law is where you want clarity. In one court case, a man (Milam) tried to redeem his $50 Federal Reserve Note in "lawful money" of the United States (gold or silver); he refused to be paid in an equivalent value in Federal Reserve Notes. The court ruled that he was "entitled to redeem his note, but not in precious metal." *Milam v. U.S.* 524 F2d 629, 630 (1974). The court cleverly evaded its responsibility and did not say what he was entitled to. No one is fooled; the court was perpetuating a fraud. If they are not redeemable, they are not notes. A Federal Reserve Note, on its face, is a fraud. Issued by a private bank it is not "federal"; there are no "reserves" as the term is colloquially understood. And now we see it is not a "note," which by definition is a promise to pay.

When you use an instrument of debt (a promissory note) for money, that note is regulated under the Uniform Commercial Code (UCC). You become a "holder" or "holder in due course" which has certain legal ramifications, and how many people want to be caught in the web of the UCC should a dispute arise about who paid who? It creates complexity where none would exist if instead you used a debt-free embodiment for money.

Private Money a Cause of War

War is a feature of private money. If society allows a privately owned entity such as a bank or banking system to issue and control money, that society is asking for war. Banks make money by loaning it to both sides:

> For both sides of a war to be loaned money from the same privately owned Central Bank is not unusual. Nothing generates debt like war. A Nation will borrow any amount to win. So naturally, ... more loans taken out, more money made by the bankers; **and even more amazing, the loans are usually given on condition that the victor pays the debts left by the loser.**[48] [emphasis added]

A nation at war needs lots of money for weapons, and if the only way for government to get it is to borrow from banks, then naturally those in political power (who would have links with the bankers) would make war in order to make loans. This is the best way for banks to make huge profits. Instead of having to make a lot of small loans, banks only have to make a few large ones, on a scale that dwarfs domestic lending, plus they are guaranteed by the full faith and credit of the government. The only way to prevent setting the stage for war is to take the profit out of it, and giving the government the power to create its own money and not borrow it is a good start.[49] [50]

As General Smedley Butler said:

> War is a racket. It always has been. It is possibly the oldest, easily the most profitable, surely the most vicious. It is international in scope. It is the only one in which the profits are reckoned in dollars and the losses in lives.

> A racket is best described, I believe, as something that is not what it seems to the majority of the people. Only a small "inside" group knows what it is about. It is conducted for the benefit of the very few, at the expense of the very many. Out of war a few people make huge fortunes.[51]

---

48   http://www.xat.org/xat/moneyhistory.html

49   The Federal Reserve Act was passed on Dec. 23, 1913; I suspect it was the bankers who wasted no time putting us into debt, by starting WW1 about half a year later, on July 28, 1914.

50   Bank funding of weapons: http://www.waronwant.org/attachments/Banking%20on %20Bloodshed.pdf

51   For a 10-page summary of General Smedley Butler's book *War is a Racket*, see http://www.wanttoknow.info/warisaracket

Unpayable Debt and Sustainability

Unpayable debt is a property of privately owned debt-money banking systems. As long as the nation can borrow more money into circulation at a rate faster than the interest due, the system will be sustainable.[52] This requires that goods and services be produced that can be used as collateral to get more loans from the banks with which to pay the interest due. This also requires that the nation's output grows exponentially since the interest due grows exponentially. Economists I have talked to understand this and use the term "sustainability," and point to the fact that for many decades our nation has experienced such growth, as if somehow exponential growth of our nation is justification for turning over that output to the banking system. However, even rabbit reproduction eventually reaches its environmental limit; nothing grows exponentially forever. But then, a society would not want to pay out the fruit of all its labor to the bankers – though from appearances I could be wrong because that is what we are doing.

To help things along, we have a "business cycle" that expands and contracts the money supply on a regular basis. When the money expands, business expands by taking loans; then the contraction occurs and businesses can't pay on the loans, forcing bankruptcies, freeing up assets to be purchased by surviving companies for pennies on the dollar to be used as collateral for new loans.

And we have deficit spending by government, which provides money to pay interest on the loans. An honest balanced budget might cause a deflation in a debt-money system and should be avoided.

As you can see, a pure debt-money system will destroy a society. It is essential that debt-free money be created and spent into circulation in order to pay the interest due, to prevent the annual compounding and exponential growth of debt that leads to societal slavery and universal poverty. The dark powers should be congratulated; they have people believing that spending money into circulation is inflationary and toxic. The key to their chains is in plain sight, and they have been led to believe it is poison.

On Getting What We Deserve

The universe is run by one law and one law only, as it relates to human affairs: *As you sow, so shall you reap*. You are free to act, but the reaction is fixed.

---

52   See Appendix A.

This law must be kept in mind when we consider usury, because the law operates such that if you steal you will be stolen from. Our society has evolved to the point that we know that stealing is wrong, and our laws forbid and punish theft. On the question of right versus wrong, right, by definition, is natural law, and wrong is counter to natural law. Anything that is wrong has a natural and unavoidable consequence. Running a stop sign where there is no traffic, whether or not you get caught, is not wrong, just prohibited. There is no natural penalty. When you steal, whether or not you get caught, you have taken the fruit of another's labor, and Nature will set it up such that someone else will steal from you.

With this understanding it becomes important to structure society so that the population does not steal. We need to weed out institutionalized stealing, because if the population steals, the population will be stolen from, and that is exactly what we see in the design of our monetary system. We are getting what we deserve. Society must stop stealing before it can expect to stop being stolen from. This something-for-nothing must end.

The ultimate theft might be considered to be slavery, and the price for enslaving someone is to be enslaved yourself. If, through the process of usury, you have "earned" a living (which necessarily is at the expense of others), you have to expect that at some time in the future you will be made to work to support others. The laws of nature cannot be deceived; a reaction will come.[53]

To try to fix our monetary system without first abolishing usury, is like trying to remove the effect without first removing the cause. Your results will be limited.

Why is usury a theft? Because those who have money put it into a bank and earn interest, and thereby live off the productive efforts of others without producing anything themselves. The concept that you are entitled to compensation for the loss of use of your money sounds perfectly reasonable, but reason needs to look deeper at all the effects on society to find the motivation to outlaw it. People know that stealing is wrong, they just haven't made the connection that something-for-nothing is theft. They have been sold on the concept that lenders are entitled to compensation for the use of their money, not realizing that it is a string of words without substance, that buying into this concept costs our nation half a trillion dollars a year.

---

53 Justice is natural law; you never get away with anything, effects always follow from causes, reactions from actions. You, and no one else, are responsible for your misery. Our nation is getting exactly what it deserves; the massive theft structured in our monetary system is the reaction to past action, whatever that action may have been.

What Do We Do Now?

As a practical matter, it doesn't look like the banks will ever be nationalized. But remember the Berlin wall. No one thought it would ever come down, but one day it did. And nationalizing the banks may not be necessary. If federal, state, or local governments charter their own banks creating debt-free money in whatever embodiment, and accept it in payment of taxes (which is what gives it value), competition will force the banks to change or die; why would you pay $150,000 interest for a bank loan, when you can get the same loan from your local treasury for $10,000? This is how the early Church prevented usury, by giving interest-free loans which took the profit out of it.

Now that you know the cause of the problem, support the cause of change – you now have the knowledge to determine what change will promote prosperity, and what will deepen the nation's poverty.

Finally, in case it isn't apparent, the monetary mess we are in is not by accident, blundering, incompetence, or stupidity, but by careful and incredibly competent design. To learn more, I would suggest starting with *Secrets of the Federal Reserve* at www.apfn.org/apfn/reserve.htm. For an excellent history of money, read *The Lost Science of Money* by Stephen Zarlenga[54] which argues that money is a creature of law. Watch the free video ZEITGEIST: ADDENDUM at www.zeitgeistmovie.com.

---

54 Available from www.monetary.org. He has been petitioning Congress to pass legislation which is substantially in accord with what I teach here, a debt-free fiat currency, and Congressman Kucinich's is promoting his Historic Monetary Reform Bill HR 2990 of 2011.

About the Author

Richard Walbaum is a professional meditator, practicing an advanced form of Transcendental Meditation (www.tm.org) on the Invincible America assembly whose purpose is to raise the collective consciousness of the U.S. by enlivening natural law through the group dynamics of consciousness, so we stop making mistakes or enemies. When everyone is our friend we will be invincible, with all good for everyone, and it is unstoppable, which more and more will manifest by people booing the government. The author can be reached at www.NaturalLawRemedy.com.

Appendix A: Is a Debt-Money System Sustainable?

This chapter is very technical and is not necessary to understand the problem of usury so is placed in an appendix.

We now look at the concept of "sustainability," a concept economists apply to debt money systems to see if they will operate over a long period of time.

Even though the debt rises exponentially, some economists believe that a debt-money system can still work; they call such a system "sustainable." In order for a monetary system to be sustainable (which means it will not crash), the output of the nation must be able to pay the interest on the debt. Since the debt rises exponentially, this means the output must also grow exponentially, at a rate that equals or exceeds the growth of interest due on the debt. Note that in a sustainable system, the debt will still rise exponentially (the characteristic of a debt-money system); it's just that the output must rise exponentially as well to meet the interest demands.

In order to pay the annual interest, new money must be created and loaned into circulation because the interest demanded in law does not exist in fact. In order to get the loans, the nation must have collateral to back the loans; the collateral comes from the increased output of the nation.[55]

We will assume in this example that Gross National Product (GNP) does not grow from year to year; we will account for growing GNP later.[56] Let's start with a money supply of $10 Billion (B) which is loaned into circulation by the banking system, which is also $10B of bank debt, and $10B in collateral is pledged to the banks from borrowers assets. Over the year, GNP is $67B; this figure is chosen to make the numbers easy to work with.[57]

At the end of the year, 10% interest on $10B of debt is $1B, bringing the debt to $11B. To collateralize this additional $1B, only $1B of the $67B output of the nation needs to be collateralized. This is a small amount, and no one would experience any problem in the first year or first decade of operation.

---

55 We will assume that the Fed will provide as much money as needed and will not create a recession by creating a shortage of money.

56 The GNP, as a measure of the nation's output, is determined by how often money changes hands in buying and selling products and services. This is the velocity times the money supply. Velocity is typically about 6, which means that over a year, a dollar finds its way into 6 different hands. See Economics, Byrns and Stone, Scott, Foresman and Company, Glenview, Illinois 1981, p. 300.

57 For a typical velocity of about 6, and a money supply of $10 B, the GNP would be 6 X 10 or $60 B; I used $67 B for ease of later computation.

Let's look at another case after 20 years; the debt has compounded to $67B and is the same size as the GNP.[58] The money supply remains unchanged. Over the years, $67B in assets have gradually been pledged as collateral for the debt so there was no hardship. Now, 10% interest on the debt is $6.7B which is 10% of the GNP. People may not notice any problem yet; the required interest payment to the banks is still only 10% of the total output. However, since 10% of the GNP is used to pay interest (a business expense), this cost is added to the price of goods. Prices will be rising.

Let's look at what happens the 21st year. The $67B compounds to $74B, an increase of $7B.[59] An additional $7B in collateral is required. In the very first year, the banks received $1B of pledged assets; in the 21st year, the banks received $7B. The economy has not changed any; the money supply is the same, and the output is the same. What have the banks done in 21 years to deserve seven times the collateral? These obligations to the bank are real; if payment is not made, the banks get to keep the collateral.

Now let's look at what happens in the 44th year when the debt is $670B, ten times the GNP.[60] At the end of the year, 10% interest must be paid on $67B which will increase the debt by $67B. This requires an additional $67B in collateral. At this point, the total output of the nation is pledged as collateral. The next year, the total GNP would not be sufficient to collateralize the loans. At this time, any free assets left in the nation must be collateralized, leaving the entire nation in mortgage. Once the collateral is used up, there can be no new loans to pay the required interest (unless banks are willing to make unsecured loans).

The conclusion is that if the GNP remains constant (doesn't grow each year), the system is not-sustainable. When the interest rate exceeds the rate of increase of GNP, unpledged assets of the nation will be used up faster than new assets are being created. When the time comes that all the assets of the nation are pledged, a great wave of bankruptcies will take place. At this point, the banking system will own all the wealth of the nation.

Since interest today[61] exceeds the growth of GNP (which is about 3%), the solution as implemented by economists, is to have a business cycle. By contracting and expanding the money supply on a cyclical basis, business are regularly forced into

---

58 D = P(1+r)n = $10 B (1+0.1)20 = $67 B. D = debt at the end of the year; P = principal borrowed; r = interest rate (10% is 0.1); n = number of years. This is the compound interest formula.
59 67 B X 1.1 = $74 B
60 $10 B (1+0.1)44 = $663 B; round it up to $670 B.
61 This book was originally published in 1992.

bankruptcy.[62] The more solvent businesses can buy the bankruptcies up at 2 cents on the dollar. These acquired assets become the collateral for new loans.

What if we try to make this system work by making the rate of growth of assets (i.e., the growth of the GNP) equal to the interest rate? Then new collateral would always be available to borrow money to pay the required interest payments.

Let's spare ourselves a detailed explanation. I will discard this unworkable approach for more general reasons. Productivity cannot grow exponentially forever.[63] Nothing in creation (that I know of) grows exponentially forever. Even bacteria will stop growing when it reaches the limit of its food supply.[64] World output will eventually reach its limit. Even if it could grow indefinitely, would we want to mortgage it all to the bankers for the sake of making a debt-money system work? Plus, everything produced must be bought and consumed; with exponential growth of commodities, eventually everyone will have what they want and stop buying.

From every angle that I look at it, I can't make a debt-money system work that is free of the evils of recession, bankruptcies, rising prices, profits from other's labor, etc. The only benefit of such a system is to those with a design to enslave the world.

We are now at the point in 2012 where the banksters are crashing the economies of all the countries of the world. This is the endpoint of the debt-money system; the banksters are foreclosing on the whole world.

---

62 The only way to stop debt from following the compound interest formula is to force people to default on their loans. The banks go under as well when people default on their debts, which explains why we have many bank and savings and loan failures today.

When the banks call their loans they destroy the money supply by canceling the demand deposits. They thus increase the purchasing power of money in terms of stocks, property, and commodities. Thus the banks impair and diminish the value of their own securities and impair the solvency of their own borrowers, thereby bringing ruin upon themselves and upon the industry and commerce of the country. [Robert Owen, National Economy and the Banking System, Senate Document #23, 1939, p. 14.]

63 Economists at a local university argued with me that output has historically grown exponentially for over 100 years. I was amazed that they would even attempt to defend this system. Why would they want or accept the growth of debt at an exponential rate?

64 I have been told that when bacteria and rabbits multiply beyond their food supply, their population also crashes.

www.ingramcontent.com/pod-product-compliance
Lightning Source LLC
Chambersburg PA
CBHW081621170526
45166CB00009B/3057